MW01537634

This book belongs to

---

the Girl Boss

Made in the USA
Las Vegas, NV
10 December 2022

61706649R00070